Harmonizing Excellence

A Symphony of Workforce Optimization

DINESH D. MAJUMDAR

Contents

Chapter 1: Unleashing the Power of Teamwork

1.1 The Secret to Supercharging Your Team

Imagine you have a superpower that can make your team stronger, faster, and smarter. Well, that superpower is called "Workforce Optimization." In this chapter, we're going to explore how you can unlock this incredible ability to boost your team's performance to a whole new level.

Close your eyes for a moment and imagine this: you're standing at the helm of a team that can achieve the extraordinary. Each member is like a superhero with their unique strengths, ready to conquer challenges and reach new heights. Now, open your eyes and know that this isn't just a dream – it's a reality waiting to be unlocked through the incredible superpower known as "Workforce Optimization."

Think of it as a secret formula that has the magical ability to make your team stronger, faster, and smarter than ever before. Just like how a superhero becomes invincible when they discover their true potential, your team too can become a force to be reckoned with.

In the pages of this chapter, we embark on a thrilling journey to unveil the true essence of this superpower. We'll dive deep into the art of Workforce Optimization, revealing its hidden facets and untapped potential. Picture yourself as the master of this ancient and powerful skill, able to infuse your team with unmatched efficiency, seamless coordination, and breathtaking productivity.

As we delve further, you'll learn the secrets of harnessing Workforce Optimization's energy to catapult your team's performance to heights you never thought possible. Just like a superhero donning their cape, you'll cloak your team with the aura of invincibility, ensuring they are always ready to conquer any challenge that comes their way.

Get ready, because by the end of this book, you'll hold in your hands the key to unlocking a realm of possibilities. It's time to awaken the dormant superpower within your team and lead them towards a future where success knows no bounds. The journey starts now, and the excitement is palpable as we unveil the secret to supercharging your team through the art of Workforce Optimization.

1.2 The Amazing Benefits of Using Your Team's Superpower

Think of your team like a team of superheroes. When they work together at their best, they can achieve amazing things! We'll discover all the cool advantages of making sure every team member is used in the best way possible. It's like creating the perfect superhero squad that can tackle any challenge.

Picture this: your team, a league of extraordinary individuals, each possessing a unique superpower. When these powers combine, they become an unstoppable force capable of achieving the most astounding feats. Just like the Avengers or the Justice League, your team has the potential to accomplish truly incredible things.

In the upcoming pages, we're about to embark on a journey that reveals the awe-inspiring benefits of harnessing your team's collective superpower, known as Workforce Optimization. Imagine every team member contributing their exceptional skills in perfect harmony, like a symphony of heroes working together to achieve a common goal.

As we explore these remarkable advantages, you'll witness the transformation that occurs when every member is utilized to their fullest potential. It's like assembling the ultimate superhero squad, where each hero's abilities complement and enhance one another. With Workforce Optimization as your guide, you'll be crafting a team that's not only highly efficient but also adaptable, ready to face any challenge with unwavering determination.

Prepare to be amazed as we unravel the threads of possibility. From increased productivity to seamless teamwork, from elevated creativity to streamlined efficiency – the benefits of utilizing your team's superpower are boundless. It's time to witness the magic that happens when every member's talents align to create a symphony of success.

By the time you reach the end of this exploration, you'll have a deep appreciation for the wonders that await. You'll hold in your hands the key to transforming your team into an assembly of champions, ready to conquer the world with their collective brilliance. So, get ready to discover how tapping into your team's superpower can lead to a future of unparalleled accomplishments. The journey is about to begin, and the possibilities are nothing short of extraordinary.

1.3 The Epic Quest: Overcoming Challenges to Unleash Your Team's Potential

Every hero faces obstacles on their journey, and so does your team. We'll dive into the difficulties that might come up when trying to make your team work at its very best. But don't worry, just like heroes always find a way, we'll learn how to conquer these challenges and make your team unstoppable.

So get ready for an adventure that will show you how to make your team a force to be reckoned with. It's time to turn your team into a supercharged dream team.

Close your eyes and imagine the heroes of old, embarking on epic quests filled with challenges and trials. Just as they faced daunting obstacles, so too does your team on its journey towards greatness. In this chapter, we plunge headfirst into the labyrinth of challenges that may thwart your team's path to excellence.

Brace yourself, for we shall confront these hurdles with unyielding resolve and unwavering determination. As heroes rise above adversity, so too shall your team ascend to conquer the obstacles that stand in their way. Remember, every setback is a chance to showcase true heroism.

Through these pages, we'll unravel the tangled webs of difficulty that may impede your team's progress. We'll unearth the barriers that threaten to hinder efficiency and harmony. But fear not! With every challenge, there lies an opportunity to shine, to innovate, and to rise above limitations.

As we delve into strategies and insights, you'll learn how heroes have always found a way, and your team will be no different. Armed with wisdom, you'll chart a course through the storm, guiding your team towards victory. Just like heroes emerge triumphant, you'll discover how to navigate the challenges and emerge stronger, more united, and unstoppable.

So, my friend, ready yourself for an odyssey of transformation, for the trials we face today will forge the champions of tomorrow. The adventure ahead will equip you with the tools and knowledge needed to transform your team into a force that cannot be ignored. It's time to embark on a journey of empowerment, turning your team into a dream team of unrivaled excellence. Prepare to emerge victorious, for the journey has begun, and the challenges will only make your triumph all the more remarkable.

Chapter 2: Workforce Analysis and Planning

2.1 Conducting a thorough analysis of existing workforce capabilities and skills

2.1.a The Canvas of Potential

Imagine you're an artist about to create a masterpiece. But instead of colors, you're working with talents and skills. In this section, we'll delve into the art of analyzing your team's unique abilities. Just like an artist studies their canvas before painting, you'll learn to unravel your team's hidden potential.

Example: Meet Sarah, a talented graphic designer. Through a comprehensive analysis, you discover her remarkable skill in visual storytelling. This insight prompts you to assign her to lead a high-profile branding project, allowing her to shine in her element.

2.1.b Blueprinting Success

Before you build a skyscraper, you need a blueprint. Similarly, crafting a winning team involves foreseeing the future. Learn the secrets of forecasting your team's needs based on the canvas you've unveiled. It's like having a crystal ball that predicts the skills you'll require to achieve your goals.

Case Study: Company X's HR department predicts a surge in customer support demands during the holiday season. By analyzing the current workforce, they identify a shortage of multilingual support agents. They strategically plan to upskill existing agents or hire temporary staff to bridge the gap.

2.1.c Symphony of Alignment

Just as music follows a rhythm, your team's planning should dance to the tune of your organization's goals. Discover the magic of aligning your workforce plan with your company's objectives. This harmony ensures every move your team makes is in sync with the grand symphony of success.

Example: Think of a football team. A goalkeeper's role is distinct from a striker's, yet both contribute to the team's victory. By aligning individual roles with the game plan, each player maximizes their impact, leading the team towards victory.

As you journey through this chapter, you'll realize that workforce analysis and planning is the compass guiding your team towards unparalleled achievements. The canvas of your team's potential, the blueprint of your aspirations, and the symphony of alignment – these elements will create a work of art that's both beautiful and powerful. Just like a masterpiece leaves an indelible mark, your workforce analysis and planning will lay the foundation for a future that's both triumphant and transformative. Get ready to craft your team's destiny, one stroke of analysis and one brush of planning at a time.

2.2 Forecasting future workforce needs based on business goals and projects

2.2.a A Glimpse into the Future

Imagine you're setting sail on a grand voyage. To navigate the open sea of business challenges, you need a compass that points towards your destination. In this section, we'll unveil the mystical art of forecasting – a crystal ball that helps you predict the talents your team will require.

Example: Let's say you run a bakery, and the holiday season is approaching. You know that during this time, demand for your delectable treats will skyrocket. By analyzing past data and current trends, you foresee the need for additional bakers and customer service staff to handle the rush.

2.2.b Decoding Business Goals

Just as a puzzle's pieces fit together to form a picture, your team's skills should align seamlessly with your business's ambitions. Learn the secret of deciphering your organization's goals and projects. This skill is akin to fitting the right puzzle pieces in place to create a beautiful and harmonious whole.

Case Study: Company Y plans to launch a new product line targeting the youth market. Workforce analysis reveals a gap in social media marketing skills within their team. In anticipation of the launch, they decide to provide training to existing employees or recruit individuals with specialized expertise.

2.2.c The Symphony of Preparation

Imagine you're a conductor, orchestrating a symphony. Each instrument plays a crucial role, and their harmonious collaboration creates a masterpiece. Similarly, workforce analysis and planning harmonize your team's talents with your organization's melody of success.

Example: Think of a theater preparing for a blockbuster show. From actors and stagehands to technicians and costume designers, every role is meticulously planned and staffed. Just like that, your team's future needs are anticipated and addressed, ensuring a flawless performance on the grand stage of business.

you'll be empowered to glimpse into the future, align your team's strengths with your business's dreams, and conduct a symphony of preparedness. This is more than just planning; it's a journey into the heart of your team's potential. With each forecast you make, you'll be weaving a tapestry of triumph, turning aspirations into reality and dreams into achievements. Get ready to step into the role of a visionary, guiding your team towards a future where they shine as stars in the sky of success.

2.3 Strategies for aligning workforce planning with organizational objectives

2.3.a The Dance of Purpose

Imagine your team as a constellation of stars, each shining brightly and contributing to the night sky's beauty. Now, envision aligning these stars to form a constellation that tells a story – your organization's story. In this section, we'll explore strategies that blend your team's talents seamlessly with your company's dreams.

Example: Think of a puzzle where each piece represents a team member. As you assemble the puzzle, the image reveals itself. Similarly, by aligning each team member's strengths, you'll create a powerful image of progress and success for your organization.

2.3.b Threads of Connection

Just as a spider weaves an intricate web, your team's skills must interlace with your company's objectives. Uncover the art of weaving these threads of connection, ensuring that every move your team makes resonates with your organization's heartbeat.

Case Study: In a software development company, the goal is to launch a groundbreaking app within a tight timeline. Workforce analysis identifies the need for additional programmers and testers. By aligning this demand with the company's objective, the team is rallied to meet the challenge head-on, resulting in a successful and timely app launch.

2.3.c The Symphony of Impact

Picture a grand orchestra, every instrument playing in harmony under the guidance of a skilled conductor. Similarly, your team's skills must harmonize under the baton of your organization's vision. Learn to compose this symphony of impact, where each note struck resonates with the melody of success.

Example: Imagine you're planning a charity event. Each team member brings a unique skill – from event planning to marketing. By aligning their efforts with the charitable cause, their collective impact becomes a heartwarming symphony of goodwill, leaving a lasting impression on attendees and achieving the event's objectives.

you'll discover the transformative power of aligning workforce planning with your organization's dreams. Like an artist blending colors on a canvas, you'll blend your team's talents with your company's aspirations to create a masterpiece of progress. This is more than just strategy; it's a heartfelt connection between the pulse of your team and the rhythm of your organization. Each strategy you employ will be a brushstroke that paints a picture of success, leaving an indelible mark on the canvas of achievement. Get ready to embrace the role of a maestro, guiding your team's symphony towards a future that resonates with harmony, purpose, and triumphant melodies.

Chapter 3: Effective Workforce Deployment

3.1 Matching the right people to the right tasks for improved efficiency

3.1.a The Puzzle of Precision

Imagine your team as a puzzle, each piece a unique skill waiting to find its perfect spot. Just like assembling a puzzle creates a beautiful picture, placing the right people in the right roles paints a masterpiece of efficiency. In this section, we'll unravel the secrets of this art, ensuring every team member shines in their designated spotlight.

Example: Picture a restaurant kitchen. The head chef knows which cook specializes in appetizers, who's a master at grilling, and who's a dessert wizard. By deploying each chef to their specialty, the kitchen runs like a well-choreographed dance, serving up delicious dishes with remarkable efficiency.

3.1.b Weaving a Tapestry of Synergy

Envision your team as a tapestry, where every thread contributes to the whole. To create a masterpiece, you must skillfully weave these threads of talent and skill together. Learn the techniques to create a harmonious blend of team members, where each one complements the strengths of others.

Case Study: In a design agency, a new project requiring both creativity and technical skills arises. By strategically deploying a team consisting of designers, programmers, and a project manager, the agency delivers a well-rounded solution that meets the client's needs and exceeds expectations.

3.1.c The Symphony of Specialization

Imagine an orchestra where each musician plays their instrument with perfection. Similarly, your team members are virtuosos in their respective domains. Discover how effective workforce deployment transforms your team into a symphony of specialization, where every note is played flawlessly, resulting in a melodious harmony of efficiency.

Example: Consider a construction project. Each worker possesses specific skills – carpentry, plumbing, electrical work. By assigning tasks according to their expertise, the project advances swiftly, and the final result is a structure built to last.

As you immerse yourself in this chapter, you'll unveil the artistry behind effective workforce deployment. Each decision you make is a brushstroke on the canvas of accomplishment, creating a portrait of efficiency and excellence. This is more than just task assignment; it's a dance of skills, a symphony of collaboration, and a display of your team's collective genius. With every example and case study, you'll gain insights into crafting a team that operates like a well-tuned instrument, producing harmonious results that resonate with achievement. Get ready to become a virtuoso conductor, leading your team's performance towards a future where each member shines, tasks are executed with precision, and success is orchestrated with unmatched brilliance.

3.2 Techniques for workload distribution and task assignment

3.2.a Crafting the Symphony of Efficiency

Imagine your team as a symphony orchestra, each member a musician playing a unique instrument. For the symphony to be harmonious, every musician must be allocated the right notes to play. In this section, we'll explore the techniques that weave together a melody of efficient workload distribution and task assignment.

Example: Visualize a software development team working on a complex project. The project manager allocates tasks based on each developer's strengths – some are excellent at coding, others at testing. As a result, the project progresses smoothly, and each team member contributes their brilliance to create a harmonious software symphony.

3.2.b The Art of Choreography

Envision your team as a dance troupe, each member performing a choreographed routine that contributes to the grand performance. Much like a choreographer carefully designs each move, you'll learn how to choreograph workload distribution, ensuring tasks are assigned in a way that maximizes efficiency.

Case Study: In a marketing agency, a new campaign is launched. The workload is divided strategically among team members based on their strengths – creative minds handle design, while analytical minds tackle data analysis. This thoughtful distribution results in a campaign that not only captures attention but also achieves measurable results.

3.2.c Sculpting Success with Precision

Imagine you're a sculptor crafting a masterpiece from blocks of stone. Each chisel stroke shapes the sculpture's form and beauty. Similarly, by mastering techniques of task assignment, you'll sculpt a team that works in perfect synchronization, chiseling away inefficiencies and revealing the masterpiece of success.

Example: Think of a restaurant during peak hours. The manager assigns experienced servers to handle busy sections, ensuring efficient service. Simultaneously, less experienced staff focus on support tasks, allowing the entire team to function cohesively, providing a memorable dining experience for patrons.

As you immerse yourself in this chapter, you'll uncover the secrets of effective workload distribution and task assignment. Each technique is a brushstroke on the canvas of accomplishment, creating a vibrant picture of efficiency and achievement. This is more than just task management; it's the creation of a dynamic, well-orchestrated team that produces results beyond expectations. With every example and case study, you'll gain insights into choreographing a team performance that dazzles with its precision and synchronicity. Get ready to step into the role of a conductor and choreographer, guiding your team's dance towards a future where tasks are executed flawlessly, goals are achieved with finesse, and success becomes a mesmerizing masterpiece.

3.3 Cross-training and upskilling employees to enhance versatility

3.3.a The Power of Versatility

Imagine your team as a group of versatile performers, each skilled in multiple acts of a grand circus. Just as a circus artist amazes with various talents, your team can dazzle with versatility. In this section, we'll explore how cross-training and upskilling can transform your team into a troupe of multi-talented performers.

Example: Visualize a retail store where employees are trained in different departments – from cashiering to inventory management. This empowers them to seamlessly switch roles, ensuring smooth operations even during busy periods and providing customers with exceptional service.

3.3.b Crafting a Multifaceted Ensemble

Envision your team as a mosaic, each member a unique piece that contributes to the larger picture. By cross-training and upskilling, you're adding new colors and patterns to the mosaic. Learn how to create a diverse ensemble where team members can confidently step into different roles, enriching the overall composition.

Case Study: In a technology company, employees are trained not only in their core areas but also exposed to related fields. A developer, for instance, may undergo upskilling in project management. This approach enhances teamwork, facilitates smoother collaborations, and allows team members to contribute beyond their original roles.

3.3.c Sculpting the Future: A Resilient Team

Imagine you're a sculptor molding clay into a shape that can adapt to various forms. Similarly, cross-training and upskilling mold your team into a resilient entity that can flexibly respond to changing demands. Discover how this approach sculpts a team that can navigate challenges with grace and mastery.

Example: Consider a healthcare setting where nurses are trained not just for their specialized roles but also in basic administrative tasks. During emergencies or high patient load, these nurses seamlessly switch to administrative duties, ensuring smooth operations while still maintaining their primary care giving responsibilities.

As you delve into this chapter, you'll uncover the transformative potential of cross-training and upskilling. Each technique is a stroke of empowerment, adding depth and richness to your team's capabilities. This isn't just about learning new skills; it's about creating a team that is adaptable, confident, and prepared to take on any role to achieve success. With every example and case study, you'll witness the evolution of a team that embraces growth and thrives in the face of change. Get ready to become a sculptor of potential, shaping your team into a resilient masterpiece that can conquer challenges and achieve greatness from every angle.

Chapter 4: Agile Scheduling and Flexibility

4.1 Implementing flexible work arrangements to accommodate varying workloads

4.1.a The Dance of Adaptation

Imagine your team as graceful dancers, moving in perfect harmony with the rhythm of work demands. Just as dancers adjust their steps to the music, your team can adjust their schedules to match varying workloads. In this section, we'll explore the art of implementing flexible work arrangements that allow your team to adapt and thrive.

Example: Picture a marketing agency handling multiple client campaigns. During peak times, team members can opt for flexible hours – some work early mornings, while others work late nights. This dynamic schedule ensures that clients receive top-notch service, no matter the time zone.

4.1.b The Canvas of Flexibility

Envision your team as artists, painting a canvas that changes colors based on the needs of the moment. Flexible work arrangements are like brushstrokes that can be adjusted to create a masterpiece of productivity. Learn how to craft a schedule that not only meets work demands but also enhances employee well-being.

Case Study: A tech startup offers remote work options for its developers. This flexibility empowers them to choose hours that align with their peak productivity, resulting in higher quality code and increased job satisfaction.

4.1.c Shaping Tomorrow: Thriving in Flux

Imagine your team as skilled navigators, steering a ship through changing tides. Flexible work arrangements equip your team with the tools to navigate uncertainties with finesse. Discover how this approach shapes a workforce that remains resilient and adaptable, no matter the challenges.

Example: Consider a customer service team that experiences fluctuations in call volume. By allowing team members to adjust their schedules based on anticipated call spikes, the company ensures exceptional service during high-demand periods, fostering customer satisfaction and loyalty.

As you delve into this chapter, you'll unveil the transformative potential of agile scheduling and flexibility. Each technique is a brushstroke on the canvas of adaptability, creating a portrait of a team that is responsive, engaged, and motivated. This isn't just about adjusting hours; it's about fostering an environment where both work and personal needs are harmoniously balanced. With every example and case study, you'll witness the evolution of a team that embraces change and thrives in a dynamic landscape. Get ready to become an architect of time, designing a schedule that empowers your team to navigate challenges with grace, achieve success, and revel in the freedom to excel.

4.2 Strategies for managing remote and distributed teams effectively

4.2.a The Boundless Horizon

Imagine your team as explorers, embarking on a journey across vast landscapes. Just as explorers conquer distant terrains, your team can conquer challenges regardless of their physical location. In this section, we'll delve into the strategies that enable you to manage remote and distributed teams with unparalleled effectiveness.

Example: Visualize a tech company with developers spread across different countries. By utilizing virtual collaboration tools and fostering open communication, the team successfully collaborates on projects, harnessing the power of diversity and expertise.

4.2.b The Tapestry of Connection

Envision your team as weavers, intertwining threads of expertise and ideas across distances. Strategies for remote team management are like the loom that creates a tapestry of collaboration, binding team members together regardless of where they are located.

Case Study: A multinational corporation manages a distributed sales team. Through regular video conferencing, training webinars, and shared digital platforms, team members exchange insights and experiences, creating a global knowledge-sharing network that boosts sales performance.

4.2.c Navigating the Digital Seas

Imagine your team as a fleet of ships, sailing together despite being scattered across oceans. Navigating the digital seas requires specialized tools and techniques. Discover how to steer your remote team towards success using technology, communication, and innovative practices.

Example: Think of a content creation agency with writers and editors working remotely. By implementing a robust content management system and conducting regular video meetings, the team ensures seamless collaboration, efficient content production, and timely delivery.

As you delve into this chapter, you'll uncover the art of managing remote and distributed teams with precision and finesse. Each strategy is a compass guiding your team's journey, creating a roadmap to success that transcends physical boundaries. This isn't just about technology; it's about building a connected, engaged, and productive team that thrives regardless of geographical constraints. With every example and case study, you'll witness the evolution of a team that embraces the digital age, excels in virtual collaboration, and achieves remarkable results. Get ready to become a captain of connectivity, steering your remote team towards victory, navigating challenges, and discovering the boundless potential of agile freedom.

4.3 Leveraging technology for dynamic scheduling and real-time adjustments

4.3.a The Digital Baton

Imagine your team as a symphony orchestra guided by a digital conductor. Just as a conductor directs each instrument to create a harmonious melody, technology can guide your team towards dynamic scheduling and real-time adjustments. In this section, we'll explore how to harness the power of technology to orchestrate a masterpiece of flexible scheduling.

Example: Picture a retail store with an automated system that adjusts staff schedules based on real-time foot traffic data. During busy periods, additional employees are scheduled on-the-fly, ensuring optimal customer service and maximizing sales.

4.3.b The Canvas of Possibilities

Envision your team as artists with a digital palette, each stroke of technology adding vibrant hues to your scheduling canvas. Discover the array of technological tools available for dynamic scheduling and adjustments, allowing you to create a work of art that is both efficient and adaptable.

Case Study: A healthcare facility employs a cloud-based scheduling software. Nurses, doctors, and support staff access the system to adjust their shifts in real-time. This flexibility not only accommodates staff preferences but also ensures adequate coverage, resulting in streamlined patient care.

4.3.c Navigating the Technological Symphony

Imagine your team as navigators on a high-tech ship, sailing through the seas of real-time adjustments. Learn to read the digital compass, steer the ship, and adapt swiftly to changing tides. Explore the strategies that transform technology into a tool for dynamic scheduling, ensuring your team sails smoothly even in turbulent waters.

Example: Think of an IT project team with members working across different time zones. A project management tool allows them to set milestones, track progress, and adjust deadlines in real-time. This ensures efficient collaboration, timely project completion, and client satisfaction.

As you immerse yourself in this chapter, you'll unveil the transformative potential of leveraging technology for dynamic scheduling and real-time adjustments. Each technological tool is a note in the symphony of efficiency, creating a melody of adaptability and success. This isn't just about software; it's about orchestrating a team that can pivot, adjust, and thrive amidst changing circumstances. With every example and case study, you'll witness the evolution of a team that embraces innovation, harnesses technology, and achieves excellence in real-time. Get ready to become a conductor of efficiency, using technology as your baton to guide your team towards a future where scheduling is seamless, adjustments are swift, and success is a harmonious blend of human and technological mastery.

Chapter 5: Performance Metrics and Measurement

5.1 Identifying key performance indicators (KPIs) for workforce utilization

5.1.a The Beacon of Insight

Imagine your team as explorers in a vast landscape, each step guided by a shining beacon. Just as explorers rely on beacons to find their way, your team relies on performance metrics to navigate towards excellence. In this section, we'll delve into the art of identifying key performance indicators (KPIs) that illuminate the path to optimal workforce utilization.

Example: Picture a sales team where performance is measured not just by revenue but also by the number of leads generated and customer satisfaction scores. By tracking these KPIs, the team gains a holistic view of their effectiveness and can adjust strategies accordingly.

5.1.b The Canvas of Measurement

Envision your team as artists, each brushstroke of data painting a vivid picture of their accomplishments. Learn how to create a canvas of measurement, where KPIs provide a detailed and comprehensive view of workforce utilization, allowing you to identify strengths, weaknesses, and areas for improvement.

Case Study: A manufacturing company monitors production output, defect rates, and employee training hours as KPIs for workforce utilization. By analyzing this data, they identify a correlation between specific training programs and reduced defects, leading to improved efficiency and product quality.

5.1.c Crafting a Symphony of Growth

Imagine your team as composers, creating a symphony of improvement with every note of data. Discover how KPIs act as musical notes, forming a harmonious melody of progress and achievement. Explore strategies for using these metrics to orchestrate a team that continually evolves and excels.

Example: Think of a customer service team that tracks KPIs such as average response time, first-contact resolution rate, and customer feedback scores. By continuously monitoring and analyzing these metrics, the team identifies opportunities to streamline processes, enhance customer interactions, and boost overall satisfaction.

As you delve into this chapter, you'll uncover the transformative potential of performance metrics and measurement. Each KPI is a data-driven brushstroke, creating a portrait of your team's effectiveness and impact. This isn't just about numbers; it's about gaining insights that guide your team towards higher levels of achievement. With every example and case study, you'll witness the evolution of a team that thrives on data-driven decision-making, continuously refines its strategies, and achieves excellence with a precision that only measurement can provide. Get ready to become a conductor of growth, using KPIs as your musical notes to guide your team's symphony towards a future where performance is optimized, progress is constant, and success is a beautifully orchestrated composition of brilliance.

5.2 Monitoring and tracking employee productivity and task completion

5.2.a The Lighthouse of Insight

Imagine your team sailing toward a distant shore, guided by the steady beam of a lighthouse. Just as sailors rely on the lighthouse's light, your team relies on performance metrics to steer toward productivity and success. In this section, we'll explore the art of monitoring and tracking employee productivity and task completion as the guiding light toward optimal performance.

Example: Visualize a software development team utilizing a project management tool that tracks tasks, progress, and deadlines. By monitoring these metrics, the team identifies bottlenecks, allocates resources efficiently, and ensures on-time project delivery.

5.2.b The Canvas of Progress

Envision your team as artists, each brushstroke of data capturing a moment of achievement. Learn how to create a canvas of progress, where metrics illustrate the journey from task initiation to completion. Discover how tracking individual and team progress fosters a culture of accountability and continuous improvement.

Case Study: A customer support team uses ticketing software to monitor response times, issue resolution rates, and customer feedback. By analyzing these metrics, the team identifies areas for improvement, leading to reduced response times and enhanced customer satisfaction.

5.2.c Orchestrating Growth and Mastery

Imagine your team as conductors, guiding an orchestra of tasks towards a harmonious symphony of accomplishment. Dive into strategies for using metrics as your baton, orchestrating a team that thrives on clear goals, data-driven insights, and a commitment to excellence.

Example: Think of a marketing team launching a new campaign. By tracking metrics such as website traffic, click-through rates, and conversion rates, the team gains a deep understanding of campaign effectiveness. This insight allows them to make real-time adjustments to optimize results and drive greater ROI.

As you immerse yourself in this chapter, you'll unveil the transformative potential of monitoring and tracking employee productivity and task completion. Each metric is a brushstroke on the canvas of progress, creating a portrait of your team's achievements and potential. This isn't just about numbers; it's about fostering a culture of transparency, ownership, and continuous growth. With every example and case study, you'll witness the evolution of a team that thrives on data, leverages insights, and achieves excellence with unwavering precision. Get ready to become a steward of achievement, using metrics as your guiding light to lead your team towards a future where tasks are completed seamlessly, goals are met consistently, and success shines brightly on the horizon of accomplishment.

5.3 Data-driven decision-making to optimize workforce allocation

5.3.a The Data Symphony

Imagine your team as conductors, wielding the baton of data to orchestrate a symphony of precision. Just as a conductor harmonizes instruments, you can use data-driven decision-making to fine-tune your workforce allocation. In this section, we'll explore how data empowers you to lead your team towards optimal allocation.

Example: Visualize a sales team analyzing data to identify peak sales hours. By allocating more staff during these hours, the team maximizes customer engagement and revenue.

5.3.b The Canvas of Insight

Envision your team as artists, each brushstroke of data adding depth and clarity to your canvas of workforce strategies. Learn how to create a canvas of insight, where data-driven decisions paint a vivid picture of efficiency and productivity.

Case Study: An e-commerce company uses data analytics to optimize warehouse staffing. By analyzing order patterns, they adjust workforce allocation to match demand, reducing wait times and enhancing customer satisfaction.

5.3.c Crafting a Symphony of Efficiency

Imagine your team as composers, crafting a symphony where data-driven decisions harmonize to create a melody of efficiency. Discover strategies for collecting, interpreting, and applying data to align workforce allocation with organizational goals.

Example: Think of a healthcare facility using patient admission data to allocate nursing staff based on anticipated patient arrivals. This foresight ensures quality care and minimizes wait times.

As you delve into this chapter, you'll unlock the transformative potential of data-driven decision-making for workforce optimization. Each data point is a note in the symphony of efficiency, painting a portrait of a team that thrives on precision, embraces insights, and achieves greatness through the symphony of data-guided allocation. This isn't just about numbers; it's about utilizing data as a compass, guiding your team towards a future where resources are allocated with finesse, outcomes are optimized, and success is a masterpiece of data-driven brilliance. With every example and case study, you'll witness the evolution of a team that leverages data as a powerful tool, navigates challenges with confidence, and achieves excellence through the symphony of data-guided allocation. Get ready to become the conductor of efficiency, using data-driven decision-making to guide your team towards a future where clarity reigns, impact is magnified, and success is a masterpiece of insightful brilliance.

Chapter 6: Employee Engagement and Motivation

6.1 Creating a positive work environment to enhance employee morale

6.1.a The Garden of Positivity

Imagine your team as a vibrant garden, where each employee is a unique flower. Just as a well-tended garden blooms with beauty, your team flourishes in a positive work environment. In this section, we'll delve into the art of creating a workplace that nurtures employee morale and cultivates a culture of engagement and motivation.

Example: Picture a company that prioritizes open communication, transparent decision-making, and recognition programs. Employees feel valued and supported, leading to increased morale, job satisfaction, and a sense of belonging.

6.1.b The Symphony of Appreciation

Envision your team as musicians in a grand symphony, each note of appreciation adding depth to the melody of motivation. Discover how acknowledging and celebrating employee contributions fosters a harmonious work environment that resonates with enthusiasm and dedication.

Case Study: A manufacturing plant implements a "Employee of the Month" program. Through nominations and peer recognition, exceptional employees are honored and rewarded. This simple gesture creates a ripple effect, inspiring others to excel and elevating overall team spirit.

6.1.c Crafting Moments of Inspiration

Imagine your team as artists, crafting a masterpiece of motivation through meaningful experiences. Explore strategies for organizing team-building activities, workshops, and skill development sessions that inspire creativity, camaraderie, and a shared sense of purpose.

Example: Think of a tech startup that hosts monthly hackathons where employees collaborate to develop innovative ideas. This not only encourages teamwork but also sparks individual creativity, fostering a dynamic and motivated work environment.

As you immerse yourself in this chapter, you'll uncover the transformative power of creating a positive work environment that fuels employee engagement and motivation. Each action you take is a brushstroke on the canvas of team spirit, creating a portrait of a workforce that is enthusiastic, committed, and passionate. This isn't just about programs; it's about fostering a sense of belonging, empowerment, and shared accomplishment. With every example and case study, you'll witness the evolution of a team that thrives in an atmosphere of positivity, excels in collaboration, and achieves greatness with unwavering enthusiasm. Get ready to become a curator of motivation, using the colors of appreciation, recognition, and shared experiences to paint a future where employees bloom, work flourishes, and success blossoms in the garden of thriving spirits.

6.2 Recognizing and rewarding high-performing individuals and teams

6.2.a Unveiling the Constellations

Imagine your team as a sky filled with stars, each representing a high-performing individual or team. Just as constellations shine brightly in the night sky, your team's brilliance deserves to be recognized and celebrated. In this section, we'll explore the art of recognizing and rewarding those who light up the path of employee engagement and motivation.

Example: Visualize a sales team that exceeds quarterly targets. Recognizing their achievements with a celebratory team dinner not only acknowledges their hard work but also strengthens camaraderie and ignites a sense of accomplishment.

6.2.b The Symphony of Acknowledgment

Envision your team as a symphony, each note of recognition harmonizing into a melody of motivation. Learn how to orchestrate the art of acknowledging high-performing individuals and teams, creating an atmosphere where achievements are celebrated and contributions are celebrated.

Case Study: An educational institution hosts an annual "Excellence Awards" ceremony. Outstanding teachers and support staff are honored for their dedication, creativity, and positive impact on students. This event fosters pride, boosts morale, and reinforces the importance of excellence.

6.2.c Crafting Legends of Inspiration

Imagine your team as storytellers, weaving tales of success and determination. Discover the strategies for crafting recognition programs that go beyond rewards – programs that inspire, uplift, and create a culture where individuals and teams aspire to achieve greatness.

Example: Think of a marketing agency that implements a "Innovation Hero" program. Employees who contribute groundbreaking ideas are publicly recognized, inspiring others to think creatively and strive for innovation.

As you dive into this chapter, you'll uncover the transformative power of recognizing and rewarding high-performing individuals and teams. Each gesture of acknowledgment is a brushstroke on the canvas of motivation, creating a portrait of a team that feels valued, inspired, and empowered. This isn't just about rewards; it's about creating a culture of appreciation, where dedication is celebrated, and efforts are cherished. With every example and case study, you'll witness the evolution of a team that shines brighter with each acknowledgment, works cohesively towards shared goals, and achieves greatness with hearts full of pride. Get ready to become a curator of legends, using the magic of recognition to paint a future where stars are born, accomplishments are celebrated, and success is a symphony of shared inspiration.

6.3 Strategies for fostering a culture of continuous improvement and innovation

6.3.a The Garden of Growth

Imagine your team as a garden of infinite potential, where every seed of improvement and innovation has the power to flourish. Just as a garden thrives under careful cultivation, your team can thrive in a culture that fosters continuous growth and innovation. In this section, we'll explore the art of cultivating such a culture, where every member is encouraged to contribute to the garden of progress.

Example: Visualize a tech company that holds regular "Innovation Hours" where employees can pitch creative ideas and collaborate on projects outside their regular tasks. This practice not only nurtures innovation but also creates a sense of ownership and empowerment.

6.3.b The Symphony of Exploration

Envision your team as explorers on a perpetual journey of discovery. Strategies for fostering a culture of continuous improvement and innovation act as a compass guiding your team through uncharted territories of creativity and advancement.

Case Study: A retail company encourages employees to provide suggestions for improving customer experience. When an employee suggests implementing self-checkout kiosks, it leads to increased efficiency, reduced wait times, and a modern shopping experience.

6.3.c Crafting a Legacy of Excellence

Imagine your team as architects, constructing a legacy of excellence through a foundation of innovation. Discover how to design initiatives that inspire experimentation, creative problem-solving, and the sharing of insights, creating a culture that thrives on the pursuit of greatness.

Example: Think of a design studio that holds monthly "Innovation Challenges" where teams collaborate to solve real-world design problems. This approach not only fuels creativity but also promotes healthy competition and a sense of accomplishment.

As you dive into this chapter, you'll uncover the transformative power of strategies for fostering a culture of continuous improvement and innovation. Each initiative is a brushstroke on the canvas of progress, creating a portrait of a team that is driven, inspired, and always reaching for new heights. This isn't just about ideas; it's about creating an environment where innovation is valued, and every member's contribution fuels the collective pursuit of excellence. With every example and case study, you'll witness the evolution of a team that thrives on curiosity, embraces change, and achieves greatness through the unyielding spirit of continuous improvement. Get ready to become a catalyst of innovation, using strategies to ignite the spark that propels your team towards a future where growth is endless, creativity knows no bounds, and success is an ongoing symphony of inspiration.

Chapter 7: Automation and Technology Integration

7.1 Integrating automation and technology to streamline routine tasks

7.1.a The Symphony of Synergy

Imagine your team as a symphony orchestra, where humans and machines harmonize to create a masterpiece of efficiency. Just as instruments come together to produce a symphony, your team and technology can blend to orchestrate a symphony of streamlined tasks. In this section, we'll delve into the art of integrating automation and technology to create a seamless workflow.

Example: Visualize a logistics company using automated inventory management software. As goods are received and shipped, the system updates inventory levels in real-time, reducing errors, minimizing manual input, and optimizing supply chain operations.

7.1.b The Canvas of Transformation

Envision your team as artists, painting a canvas where every stroke of technology enhances the masterpiece of productivity. Learn how to create a canvas of transformation, where technology and automation serve as brushes that simplify routine tasks, allowing your team to focus on what truly matters.

Case Study: An HR department integrates an automated recruitment platform that screens resumes, conducts preliminary interviews, and shortlists candidates based on predefined criteria. This frees up HR professionals to engage in more strategic activities, ultimately improving the quality of hires.

7.1.c Forging a New Dawn

Imagine your team as explorers, embarking on a journey into the realm of innovative efficiency. Discover how the integration of automation and technology reshapes the landscape of work, enabling your team to navigate uncharted territories with a heightened sense of purpose and potential.

Example: Think of a marketing agency using AI-powered analytics tools to analyze consumer behavior and trends. By automating data analysis, the team gains actionable insights faster, enabling them to create more targeted and effective campaigns.

As you immerse yourself in this chapter, you'll unveil the transformative power of integrating automation and technology to streamline routine tasks. Each technological integration is a brushstroke on the canvas of optimization, creating a portrait of a team that is empowered, forward-looking, and committed to working smarter. This isn't just about machines; it's about creating a harmonious partnership where technology amplifies human capabilities. With every example and case study, you'll witness the evolution of a team that embraces automation, leverages technology, and achieves excellence through the symphony of seamless operations. Get ready to become a conductor of innovation, using the notes of automation and technology integration to guide your team's journey towards a future where routine tasks are effortless, creativity thrives, and success resonates in every efficient gesture.

7.2 Leveraging AI and analytics for data-driven insights into workforce utilization

7.2.a The Oracle of Insights

Imagine your team as seekers of hidden treasure, embarking on a quest for valuable insights. Just as explorers rely on ancient maps to guide their way, your team can rely on AI and analytics to navigate the intricate landscapes of workforce utilization. In this section, we'll embark on a journey to uncover the transformative power of leveraging AI and analytics for data-driven insights.

Example: Visualize a retail chain using AI-powered workforce analytics to forecast peak shopping hours. By analyzing historical data and external factors, the system predicts foot traffic, enabling the store to schedule staff accordingly, ensuring optimal customer service during busy periods.

7.2.b The Canvas of Discovery

Envision your team as artists, each stroke of AI and analytics revealing a new facet of workforce dynamics. Learn how to create a canvas of discovery, where data-driven insights paint a vivid picture of employee performance, task allocation, and utilization patterns, allowing you to make informed decisions.

Case Study: A hospitality chain utilizes analytics to study the impact of employee training on customer reviews. By correlating training data with guest feedback, the chain identifies training programs that directly contribute to enhanced customer satisfaction and loyalty.

7.2.c Crafting a Symphony of Mastery

Imagine your team as conductors of a grand symphony, with AI and analytics as the orchestra, producing harmonious melodies of understanding. Discover how to orchestrate AI and analytics tools to empower your team with the knowledge to optimize workforce utilization, driving the symphony of success.

Example: Think of a project management team using AI to analyze project timelines, resource allocation, and team performance. By identifying patterns and trends, the team can proactively address bottlenecks, allocate resources efficiently, and ensure timely project delivery.

As you dive into this chapter, you'll uncover the transformative potential of leveraging AI and analytics for data-driven insights into workforce utilization. Each insight is a spark of wisdom, lighting up the path to optimized performance and utilization. This isn't just about numbers; it's about discovering hidden gems of knowledge that empower your team to achieve more, innovate, and excel. With every example and case study, you'll witness the evolution of a team that embraces AI, harnesses analytics, and achieves mastery through the symphony of data-driven decision-making. Get ready to become a maestro of insight, using AI and analytics to lead your team towards a future where understanding is illuminated, actions are purposeful, and success resonates through the symphony of empowered utilization.

7.3 Ensuring a balance between technology and human intervention

7.3.a The Dance of Equilibrium

Imagine your team as dancers in a graceful waltz, where technology and human intervention move together in perfect harmony. Just as dancers find balance and synchrony in their steps, your team can find equilibrium between technology and the human touch in the pursuit of workforce optimization. In this section, we'll explore the art of striking the right balance, ensuring that both elements contribute to a symphony of success.

Example: Visualize a customer service center that uses AI-powered chatbots for routine inquiries, freeing up human agents to handle complex and emotionally sensitive issues. This balance ensures efficient responses while preserving the human connection for matters that require empathy.

7.3.b The Canvas of Collaboration

Envision your team as artists, collaboratively painting a canvas where technology and human intervention blend seamlessly. Learn how to create a canvas of collaboration, where both elements work together to enhance efficiency, engagement, and the overall employee experience.

Case Study: An e-commerce platform uses automated order processing for routine transactions, while maintaining a dedicated customer support team for personalized assistance. This balance between automation and human intervention results in faster order fulfillment and exceptional customer satisfaction.

7.3.c Crafting the Symphony of Synergy

Imagine your team as composers, orchestrating a symphony where technology and human intervention create a harmonious melody of optimization. Discover how to craft strategies that capitalize on the strengths of both elements, resulting in a workforce that is empowered, engaged, and uniquely positioned for success.

Example: Think of a manufacturing company that integrates IoT sensors to monitor equipment performance and maintenance needs. Technicians receive real-time alerts and use their expertise to address potential issues promptly, reducing downtime and ensuring efficient operations.

As you immerse yourself in this chapter, you'll unveil the transformative potential of ensuring a balance between technology and human intervention. Each collaboration is a note in the symphony of equilibrium, creating a portrait of a team that embraces innovation while cherishing the human connection. This isn't just about tools; it's about crafting an environment where technology amplifies human capabilities, and human intuition guides technological implementation. With every example and case study, you'll witness the evolution of a team that thrives in the delicate dance of technology and humanity, achieves excellence with a sense of purpose, and strikes a harmonious balance that resonates with success. Get ready to become a conductor of synergy, using the dual forces of technology and human intervention to guide your team's journey towards a future where efficiency is amplified, relationships are nurtured, and success is a masterpiece of collaborative brilliance.

Chapter 8: Workforce Development and Training

8.1 Designing effective training programs to enhance skills and knowledge

8.1.a The Forge of Growth

Imagine your team as artisans, each in need of nurturing to sculpt their skills into masterpieces. Just as blacksmiths shape raw metal into intricate works of art, your team's potential can be honed through effective training programs. In this section, we'll explore the art of designing training programs that ignite a fire of skill enhancement and knowledge acquisition.

Example: Visualize a software development team participating in a "Hackathon Bootcamp" where they learn to collaborate, problem-solve, and develop innovative solutions under tight deadlines. This immersive experience not only enhances technical skills but also fosters teamwork and adaptability.

8.1.b The Canvas of Transformation

Envision your team as artists, each brushstroke of training adding depth and richness to their skillset canvas. Learn how to create a canvas of transformation, where training programs empower individuals to evolve, excel, and reach new heights of proficiency.

Case Study: A healthcare institution implements a comprehensive training program for nurses that covers patient care, communication skills, and emergency response. This investment in training leads to improved patient outcomes, increased staff confidence, and a positive impact on overall healthcare quality.

8.1.c Crafting Legacies of Mastery

Imagine your team as craftsmen, carving legacies of mastery through thoughtfully designed training. Discover strategies for crafting training programs that inspire a culture of continuous learning, development, and a shared pursuit of excellence.

Example: Think of a marketing agency that offers monthly "Innovation Workshops" where employees explore emerging trends, experiment with new tools, and collaborate on cutting-edge campaigns. This ongoing training fosters a culture of creativity and positions the team as industry leaders.

As you delve into this chapter, you'll uncover the transformative power of designing effective training programs that enhance skills and knowledge. Each program is a brushstroke on the canvas of growth, creating a portrait of a team that thrives on learning, embraces challenges, and continuously evolves. This isn't just about education; it's about crafting an environment where development is celebrated, potential is unlocked, and mastery becomes the norm. With every example and case study, you'll witness the evolution of a team that embraces training, invests in growth, and achieves excellence through the symphony of continuous improvement. Get ready to become a curator of mastery, using training as your medium to guide your team towards a future where skills are sharpened, knowledge is expanded, and success is a masterpiece of cultivated brilliance.

8.2 Continuous learning initiatives for workforce growth and adaptability

8.2.a The Garden of Evolution

Imagine your team as a garden of perpetual bloom, where every seed of knowledge sown bears the fruit of growth. Just as a garden thrives through seasons of change, your team flourishes through continuous learning initiatives that nurture growth and adaptability. In this section, we'll explore the art of fostering a culture of perpetual evolution.

Example: Visualize a sales team engaging in monthly "Learning Circles" where members share success stories, challenges, and insights. This collaborative approach not only enhances skills but also encourages cross-functional learning and empathy.

8.2.b The Canvas of Resilience

Envision your team as artists, each brushstroke of new knowledge adding layers of resilience to their canvas of capabilities. Learn how to create a canvas of resilience, where continuous learning initiatives empower individuals to navigate challenges, seize opportunities, and evolve in an ever-changing landscape.

Case Study: A technology company offers employees access to online courses and certifications. An employee takes a course in a new programming language, enabling them to contribute to a cutting-edge project, showcasing the direct impact of continuous learning on business innovation.

8.2.c Crafting a Symphony of Transformation

Imagine your team as composers, crafting a symphony where each note of learning contributes to a harmonious melody of adaptability. Discover strategies for orchestrating initiatives that foster a lifelong commitment to learning, preparing your team for the dynamic demands of the future.

Example: Think of a financial institution that hosts quarterly "Innovation Challenges" where employees propose and develop creative solutions to industry challenges. By encouraging learning through innovation, the institution empowers employees to adapt to rapidly evolving financial trends.

As you delve into this chapter, you'll uncover the transformative power of continuous learning initiatives for workforce growth and adaptability. Each initiative is a note in the symphony of evolution, creating a portrait of a team that thrives on curiosity, embraces change, and celebrates the journey of learning. This isn't just about acquiring new skills; it's about cultivating a mindset of lifelong learning, where growth is celebrated, and adaptability becomes second nature. With every example and case study, you'll witness the evolution of a team that values knowledge, invests in self-improvement, and achieves excellence through the symphony of perpetual development. Get ready to become a conductor of transformation, using continuous learning initiatives to guide your team towards a future where growth is boundless, resilience is unwavering, and success is a masterpiece of evergreen brilliance.

8.3 Mentoring and coaching to empower employees for higher responsibilities

8.3.a Unleashing the Spark

Imagine your team as stars in a constellation, each with the potential to shine brighter than they ever thought possible. Just as stars receive energy from the universe to emit their radiant light, your team can receive empowerment through mentoring and coaching, propelling them towards higher responsibilities. In this section, we'll journey into the heart of transformation, where mentorship and coaching become the catalysts for brilliance.

Example: Picture a junior graphic designer paired with a seasoned mentor who guides them through complex projects, offers feedback, and instills the art of visual storytelling. Through this nurturing relationship, the mentee discovers untapped potential and grows into a creative force.

8.3.b The Canvas of Growth

Envision your team as artists, each brushstroke of guidance adding depth and vibrancy to their canvas of capabilities. Learn how to create a canvas of growth, where mentorship and coaching infuse passion, skills, and a sense of purpose, creating masterpieces of achievement.

Case Study: An architecture firm establishes a "Rising Stars Program" where aspiring architects are coached by experienced mentors. The mentorship includes real-world projects, shadowing opportunities, and presentations, allowing mentees to develop their design vision and leadership acumen.

8.3.c Crafting a Symphony of Empowerment

Imagine your team as composers, orchestrating a symphony where mentoring and coaching harmoniously blend to create a melody of empowerment. Discover strategies for crafting programs that uplift employees, foster resilience, and empower them with the skills and confidence needed to embrace higher responsibilities.

Example: Think of a sales team implementing "Leadership Accelerator Sessions" where employees are coached on negotiation tactics, effective communication, and strategic thinking. These sessions empower individuals with the tools to confidently lead complex sales engagements.

As you delve into this chapter, you'll uncover the emotional essence of mentoring and coaching as vehicles of empowerment. Each mentorship and coaching interaction is a note in the symphony of growth, painting a portrait of a team that dares to dream big, takes bold steps, and ascends to new heights of accomplishment. This isn't just about guidance; it's about igniting passion, building self-assurance, and creating an environment where each person's journey is guided by shared wisdom and support. With every example and case study, you'll witness the evolution of a team that embraces mentorship, seeks transformation, and achieves excellence through the symphony of empowered growth. Get ready to become a conductor of empowerment, using mentoring and coaching to guide your team towards a future where greatness is realized, leadership is embraced, and success is a masterpiece of illuminated brilliance.

Chapter 9: Effective Communication and Collaboration

9.1 Establishing clear communication channels for seamless coordination

9.1.a The Tapestry of Connection

Imagine your team as weavers, intertwining threads of communication to create a tapestry of unity. Just as each thread contributes to the strength of a tapestry, your team's success hinges on effective communication and collaboration. In this section, we'll explore the art of establishing clear communication channels that lead to seamless coordination.

Example: Visualize a cross-functional project team using a digital platform for real-time updates, task assignments, and feedback sharing. This unified approach ensures everyone stays informed, aligned, and engaged.

9.1.b The Canvas of Synergy

Envision your team as artists, each brushstroke of communication enhancing the vibrancy of your canvas of collaboration. Learn how to create a canvas of synergy, where communication flows effortlessly, fostering trust, creativity, and a shared sense of purpose.

Case Study: A marketing agency adopts a "Daily Huddle" practice where team members gather for a 10-minute morning meeting. This concise session promotes open dialogue, provides a platform for addressing challenges, and kickstarts the day with a unified focus.

9.1.c Crafting a Symphony of Unity

Imagine your team as composers, crafting a symphony where communication and collaboration harmonize to create a melody of unity. Discover strategies for orchestrating initiatives that promote transparent communication, encourage active listening, and foster a culture of seamless coordination.

Example: Think of a customer support team implementing a "Voice of the Customer" program, where feedback from customers is regularly collected and shared with relevant departments. This practice not only improves communication but also fuels a customer-centric approach across the organization.

As you immerse yourself in this chapter, you'll uncover the emotional essence of effective communication and collaboration. Each communication channel and collaborative effort is a note in the symphony of unity, painting a portrait of a team that thrives on connection, celebrates diversity of thought, and achieves greatness through seamless coordination. This isn't just about words; it's about building bridges of understanding, nurturing empathy, and creating an environment where each voice is heard and valued. With every example and case study, you'll witness the evolution of a team that embraces communication, fosters collaboration, and achieves excellence through the symphony of connected unity. Get ready to become a conductor of harmony, using effective communication and collaboration to guide your team towards a future where relationships are nurtured, ideas flourish, and success is a masterpiece of synchronized brilliance.

9.2 Collaborative tools and platforms to enhance cross-functional teamwork

9.2.a The Tapestry of Collaboration

Imagine your team as artisans, each weaving their unique thread into a tapestry of cross-functional harmony. Just as diverse threads come together to create a vibrant fabric, your team's success hinges on collaborative tools and platforms that enhance cross-functional teamwork. In this section, we'll explore the art of using technology to weave a tapestry of seamless collaboration.

Example: Visualize a design studio using an online project management platform where designers, writers, and marketers collaborate on campaigns. This digital hub ensures everyone contributes, tracks progress, and aligns efforts, resulting in cohesive and visually stunning campaigns.

9.2.b The Canvas of Unity

Envision your team as artists, each brushstroke of collaborative technology adding depth and richness to your canvas of teamwork. Learn how to create a canvas of unity, where collaborative tools and platforms foster creativity, inclusivity, and a shared sense of achievement.

Case Study: A healthcare network implements a secure communication app that connects doctors, nurses, and administrators in real-time. This platform facilitates instant updates on patient care, eliminates communication delays, and enhances patient outcomes.

9.2.c Crafting a Symphony of Connectivity

Imagine your team as composers, orchestrating a symphony where collaborative tools and platforms harmonize to create a melody of unity. Discover strategies for crafting initiatives that leverage technology to foster communication, streamline processes, and unlock the full potential of cross-functional collaboration.

Example: Think of a technology company using a virtual whiteboard platform where developers, QA testers, and designers can brainstorm, sketch ideas, and iterate on designs in real-time. This virtual space promotes co-creation, speeds up decision-making, and leads to innovative solutions.

As you delve into this chapter, you'll uncover the emotional essence of collaborative tools and platforms in enhancing cross-functional teamwork. Each technological integration is a note in the symphony of unity, painting a portrait of a team that thrives on shared knowledge, respects diverse expertise, and achieves greatness through seamless collaboration. This isn't just about tools; it's about fostering connections, breaking down silos, and creating an environment where cross-functional collaboration becomes a natural rhythm. With every example and case study, you'll witness the evolution of a team that embraces technology, nurtures collaboration, and achieves excellence through the symphony of unified teamwork. Get ready to become a conductor of connectivity, using collaborative tools and platforms to guide your team towards a future where creativity flows, barriers are dismantled, and success is a masterpiece of harmonious brilliance.

9.3 Overcoming communication barriers and fostering a culture of open dialogue

9.3.a Shattering the Silence

Imagine your team as explorers in a vast wilderness, each seeking to bridge the gaps that hinder their progress. Just as explorers conquer obstacles to reach uncharted territories, your team can overcome communication barriers to cultivate a culture of open dialogue. In this section, we'll embark on a journey to dismantle barriers and foster a harmonious culture of communication and collaboration.

Example: Visualize a multicultural team using regular "Cultural Exchange Sessions" to share traditions, values, and communication norms. This practice enhances understanding, reduces misunderstandings, and strengthens teamwork.

9.3.b The Canvas of Connection

Envision your team as artists, each brushstroke of open dialogue adding depth and vibrancy to your canvas of collaboration. Learn how to create a canvas of connection, where open communication is a cornerstone, fostering trust, empathy, and a shared sense of purpose.

Case Study: A global tech company establishes "Feedback Fridays," where employees provide anonymous feedback on communication challenges they face. Leadership addresses these issues, creating a safe space for dialogue and improving communication across the organization.

9.3.c Crafting a Symphony of Harmony

Imagine your team as composers, crafting a symphony where open dialogue and effective communication harmonize to create a melody of unity. Discover strategies for nurturing a culture where speaking up is encouraged, and barriers to communication are dismantled to unlock the full potential of collaboration.

Example: Think of a retail team using "Town Hall Meetings" where leadership shares updates, goals, and challenges openly. Employees are also invited to ask questions and provide insights, fostering a culture of transparency and inclusive dialogue.

As you immerse yourself in this chapter, you'll uncover the emotional essence of overcoming communication barriers and fostering open dialogue. Each act of breaking down barriers and encouraging dialogue is a note in the symphony of unity, painting a portrait of a team that values every voice, embraces diversity of thought, and achieves greatness through open collaboration. This isn't just about words; it's about creating an environment where communication is a bridge, dialogue is a melody, and understanding is a tapestry that binds the team together. With every example and case study, you'll witness the evolution of a team that champions open communication, builds bridges of understanding, and achieves excellence through the symphony of unified dialogue. Get ready to become a conductor of harmony, using open dialogue to guide your team towards a future where barriers are conquered, connections are strong, and success is a masterpiece of shared brilliance.

Chapter 10: Adapting to Changing Workforce Trends

10.1 Navigating the gig economy and freelancing trends for specialized tasks

10.1.a Section 1: Charting New Horizons

Imagine your team as sailors, navigating uncharted waters where the tides of the workforce ebb and flow in unfamiliar patterns. Just as sailors rely on their skills to navigate changing seas, your team can adapt to the dynamic gig economy and freelancing trends for specialized tasks. In this section, we'll embark on a voyage to embrace evolving workforce dynamics.

Example: Visualize a marketing agency partnering with freelance graphic designers for seasonal campaigns. This agile approach allows the agency to tap into specialized skills on-demand, ensuring creative excellence during peak workloads.

10.1.b The Canvas of Flexibility

Envision your team as artists, each brushstroke of adaptability adding depth and vibrancy to your canvas of workforce strategies. Learn how to create a canvas of flexibility, where your team seamlessly integrates freelancers and gig workers to accomplish specific tasks with precision.

Case Study: An e-commerce startup collaborates with a network of freelancers to handle customer service during peak holiday seasons. The flexible workforce ensures rapid response times, high-quality service, and customer satisfaction.

10.1.c Crafting a Symphony of Resilience

Imagine your team as composers, crafting a symphony where the gig economy and freelancing trends harmonize to create a melody of adaptability. Discover strategies for weaving freelancers and gig workers into your team's fabric, creating a symphony where diverse talents contribute to your collective success.

Example: Think of a software development team utilizing freelance QA testers for project-specific quality assurance needs. By seamlessly integrating these testers, the team maintains efficiency and delivers exceptional software quality.

As you dive into this chapter, you'll uncover the emotional essence of embracing changing workforce trends. Each adaptation to the gig economy and freelancing landscape is a note in the symphony of resilience, painting a portrait of a team that thrives on versatility, welcomes innovation, and achieves greatness through flexible collaboration. This isn't just about tasks; it's about harnessing a dynamic workforce, unlocking specialized talents, and creating a culture where agility is celebrated. With every example and case study, you'll witness the evolution of a team that embraces change, navigates complexity, and achieves excellence through the symphony of adaptable synergy. Get ready to become a conductor of resilience, using the gig economy and freelancing trends to guide your team towards a future where possibilities are endless, boundaries are pushed, and success is a masterpiece of agile brilliance.

10.2 Strategies for integrating contingent workers and freelancers into the workforce

10.2.a Welcoming the Unseen Stars

Imagine your team as constellations, where each star represents a unique skill waiting to shine. Just as constellations combine individual stars to create breathtaking night skies, your team can harness the power of contingent workers and freelancers to illuminate your workforce with diverse talents. In this section, we'll unveil the strategies to seamlessly integrate these stars into your constellation of success.

Example: Visualize a manufacturing company collaborating with specialized freelancers to design and prototype a cutting-edge product. By integrating these experts, the company accelerates innovation and brings exceptional ideas to life.

10.2.b The Mosaic of Synergy

Envision your team as artists, each brushstroke of integration adding depth and vibrancy to your mosaic of collective brilliance. Learn how to create a mosaic of synergy, where contingent workers and freelancers seamlessly join forces with your core team to accomplish shared goals.

Case Study: A digital marketing agency regularly hires social media experts as contingent workers to manage campaigns for different clients. These specialists bring fresh perspectives, drive engagement, and enhance overall campaign success.

10.2.c Crafting a Symphony of Unity

Imagine your team as composers, orchestrating a symphony where contingent workers and freelancers harmoniously blend with your core team, creating a melody of unified accomplishment. Discover strategies for weaving these skilled individuals into the fabric of your workforce, fostering a culture of collaboration, and achieving excellence.

Example: Think of a healthcare facility incorporating contingent nurses during peak patient loads. By seamlessly integrating these nurses into the care team, patient satisfaction remains high, and quality care is maintained.

As you embark on this chapter, you'll uncover the emotional essence of integrating contingent workers and freelancers. Each integration is a note in the symphony of unity, painting a portrait of a team that embraces diversity, values expertise, and achieves greatness through seamless collaboration. This isn't just about tasks; it's about embracing new perspectives, harnessing specialized skills, and creating an environment where every star contributes to the brilliance of the whole. With every example and case study, you'll witness the evolution of a team that thrives on inclusivity, celebrates unique talents, and achieves excellence through the symphony of integrated synergy. Get ready to become a conductor of unity, using contingent workers and freelancers to guide your team towards a future where boundaries are dissolved, skills are celebrated, and success is a masterpiece of collaborative brilliance.

10.3 Remaining agile in the face of evolving workforce dynamics

10.3.a Embracing the Winds of Change

Imagine your team as agile dancers, gracefully moving in sync with the rhythm of evolving workforce dynamics. Just as dancers adapt their steps to different music, your team can embrace agility to navigate the ever-changing landscape of work. In this section, we'll learn how to master the dance of agility and stay resilient in the face of shifting tides.

Example: Visualize a software development team using Agile methodologies to flexibly respond to changing project requirements. This approach ensures continuous progress and customer satisfaction, even as priorities shift.

10.3.b The Canvas of Resilience

Envision your team as artists, each brushstroke of agility adding depth and vibrancy to your canvas of adaptability. Learn how to create a canvas of resilience, where your team pivots effortlessly, seizes opportunities, and thrives amidst unpredictable changes.

Case Study: An event planning company adeptly switches from in-person to virtual events during the pandemic, showcasing the power of agility in embracing new formats and delivering exceptional experiences.

10.3.c Crafting a Symphony of Versatility

Imagine your team as composers, orchestrating a symphony where agility and flexibility harmonize to create a melody of innovation. Discover strategies for cultivating a mindset of adaptability, fostering a culture of quick response, and achieving excellence in the face of dynamic workforce dynamics.

Example: Think of a retail chain that quickly adjusts staffing levels based on seasonal demands. By seamlessly adapting to fluctuations, the company maintains customer service levels and sustains employee morale.

As you journey through this chapter, you'll uncover the emotional essence of agility in the face of evolving workforce dynamics. Each adaptation is a note in the symphony of versatility, painting a portrait of a team that welcomes change, thrives on uncertainty, and achieves greatness through the dance of agility. This isn't just about reacting; it's about embracing opportunities, cultivating resilience, and creating an environment where innovation flourishes. With every example and case study, you'll witness the evolution of a team that dances through challenges, embraces transformation, and achieves excellence through the symphony of agile brilliance. Get ready to become a conductor of versatility, using agility to guide your team towards a future where adaptability is your strength, change is your rhythm, and success is a masterpiece of dynamically brilliant achievement.

Conclusion: Sustaining Workforce Optimization

In the tapestry of business excellence, one thread stands out, woven intricately into the fabric of success - Sustaining Workforce Optimization. As we draw the final strokes on this canvas of knowledge, let us gather the jewels of wisdom we've uncovered, and string them into a necklace of strategies that shimmer with the promise of maximizing workforce utilization.

In our journey through these pages, we've discovered that every cog in the organizational machinery holds the potential to shine brighter, to contribute more, to elevate the collective endeavor. It is through the art of alignment that we unlock this potential, aligning skills and aspirations with tasks and responsibilities. And yet, alignment is not static; it is a symphony of continuous adaptation. Like the seasons, the workforce must change, evolve, and grow.

The heartbeat of sustained optimization resonates with the rhythm of continuous improvement. We've seen the power of data, harnessed to illuminate the path toward enhanced decision-making. The journey does not end when a solution is found; it flourishes through the nurturing hands of iterative refinement. It's a melody that invites experimentation, embraces failure, and dances with innovation.

But what is knowledge, if not a lantern guiding us through the uncharted territories of progress? As we put down these pages, remember that the true voyage lies beyond the final word. Implement, my dear reader, for it is in action that inspiration breathes life. The tapestry we've woven here is more than a record of ideas; it's a call to arms, a symphony of possibility, a testament to your power to shape the destiny of your workforce.

In the ever-shifting landscape of business, one thing remains constant: the pursuit of excellence. The quest for long-term workforce efficiency is not a destination; it is a pilgrimage of dedication, a commitment to weaving brilliance into the very fabric of your organization. So step boldly, armed with the knowledge gained, and let your workforce's potential unfurl like a banner in the winds of change.

Sustaining workforce optimization is not a mere aspiration; it is a legacy you sculpt with every decision, every strategy, and every heartbeat of progress. And so, as this chapter comes to a close, let the echoes of these insights reverberate in the corridors of your endeavors, and may your journey be illuminated by the radiant light of a maximized, empowered, and thriving workforce.